SAVOR LIFE
a delicious way to grow!

Author Nataliia Prokopchik
Illustrator Anastasiia Zhelik

by NataWithKids
Las Vegas, Nevada, USA

Author
Nataliia Prokopchik

Savor Life: A Delicious Way to Grow
Winter — Book 1
of the Savor Life Series

© 2025 NataWithKids LLC. All rights reserved.
No part of this book may be reproduced or transmitted in any form or by any means, electronic or mechanical, including photocopying, recording, or any information storage or retrieval system, without the prior written permission of the publisher, except in the case of brief quotations used in reviews or critical articles.

All recipes, stories, questions, activities, and other original texts
© Nataliia Prokopchik.
Certain nursery rhymes and songs in this book are reproduced from traditional works in the public domain.

ISBN: 979-8-9997729-0-9
Library of Congress Control Number: 2025920428

First edition, October 2025
Printed in the United States of America

Illustrations and cover design by Anastasiia Zhelik
Interior layout by Alexander Dubasov

Published by NataWithKids LLC
Las Vegas, Nevada
www.natawithkids.com

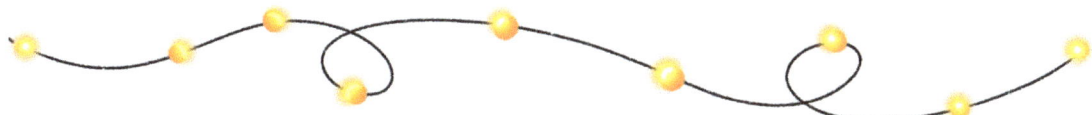

This book belongs to

To families with children who are ready to turn the kitchen into a place of warmth, growth, and delicious discoveries.

To Michael Boley — a little chef and great explorer of flavors. May you and joy find delight in every step of your culinary adventures.

Table of Contents
For Kids

Orange Cupcakes 14

Orange Cranberry Scones 16

Lemon Poppy Seed Cake 20

Gingerbread Christmas Tree 28

Christmas Wreath 40

Festive Brownies 42

Chocolate Christmas Trees 44

Christmas Wreath Shortbread Cookies 46

Chocolate Crinkle Cookies 52

Cranberry Chocolate Chip Cookies 58

Heart-Shaped Puff Pastry 60

Berry & Almond Bundt Cake 68

Tropical Winter Loaf Cake 76

🌟 And beyond the recipes... discover more than 50 additional illustrated pages with poems, riddles, conversation starters, thought-provoking questions, mazes, and other creative activities.

🌟 For Parents — practical tips, reflections, and inspiration for cooking with children.

In a cozy little house in the middle of a snowy forest lived Daddy Bear and Mommy Bear. They had a daughter named Lily and a son named Toby.

Let's continue the story together!

Good morning!

Look at Toby. How do you think he feels this morning — sleepy, happy, or excited? How can you tell?

What is one thing Toby might be thankful for right now? What is one thing you are thankful for this morning?

If you could whisper something to Toby before he gets out of bed, what would you tell him?

What do you think Toby is looking forward to today?

♪♫♪♪♫♪♫

This is the way we wash our hands,
wash our hands, wash our hands.
This is the way we wash our hands
so early in the morning.

This is the way we wash our face,
wash our face, wash our face.
This is the way we wash our face
on a cold and frosty morning.

Toby and Lily love having omelets for breakfast.
They like to add different ingredients.
Let's find the matching ingredients in the left and right columns
at the same time, using both hands!

Left hand	Right hand
cucumber	broccoli
tomato	corn
cheese	cucumber
mushroom	tomato
corn	mushroom
broccoli	cheese

What would you add to your omelet? What does your mom or dad like to add?

Let's count how many eggs are in each carton!

1 2 3 4 5 6 7 8 9 10

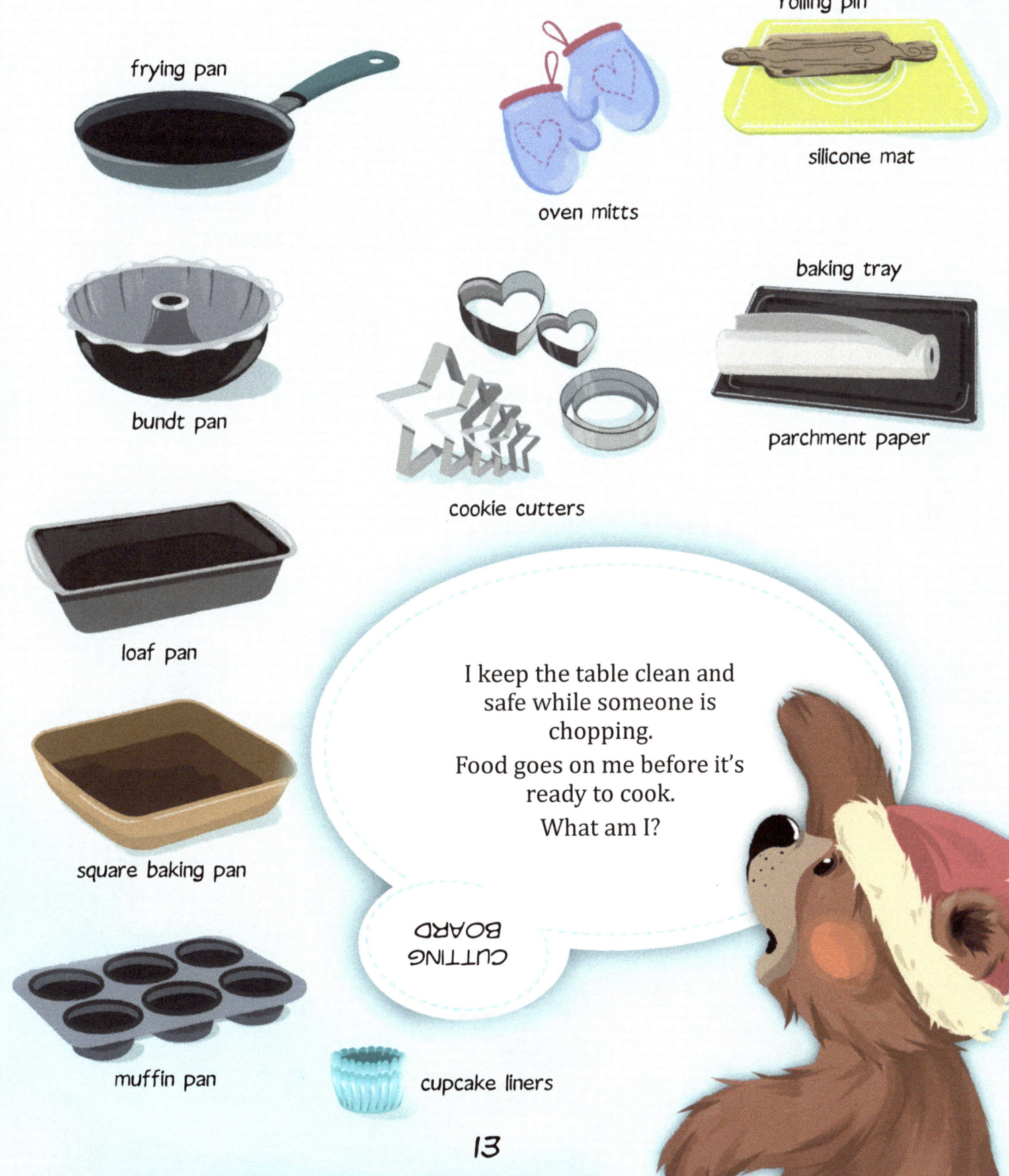

Orange Cupcakes

Ingredients (Makes 12 cupcakes):

- 1/4 cup orange juice
- zest of 1 orange
- 3/4 cup sugar
- 1/2 cup (113 g) unsalted butter, softened
- 3 eggs
- 1 1/2 cups all-purpose flour
- 1 1/2 teaspoons baking powder

Creative Process

1. Remove the butter and eggs from the fridge. Wash the orange, grate the zest, and squeeze out the juice.

2. Grease a muffin tin or line it with paper liners. Preheat the oven to 355°F.

3. In a large bowl, beat the softened butter with the sugar until smooth. Stir in the orange zest and juice.

4. In a separate bowl, beat the eggs, then pour them into the butter mixture and mix until combined.

5. Sift together the flour and baking powder, then gradually fold them into the wet ingredients with a spatula until the batter is creamy.

6. Fill each cupcake cup about two-thirds full, leaving room for the cupcakes to rise.

7. Bake for 20–25 minutes, or until a toothpick inserted into the center comes out clean.

8. Remove from the oven and let cool. Decorate as desired.

Enjoy!

Orange Cranberry Scones

Ingredients:

- zest of 1 orange
- 2 cups all-purpose flour
- 1 1/2 teaspoons baking powder
- 1/3 cup sugar
- 1/2 teaspoon salt
- 1/2 cup (85 g) cold unsalted butter, cubed
- 1/2 cup cold heavy cream
- 2/3 cup dried or fresh cranberries
- 1/3 cup chocolate chips

Creative Process

1. Wash the orange. Grate the orange zest with a fine grater.
2. In a large bowl, sift together the flour and baking powder. Stir in the sugar, salt, and orange zest.
3. Cut the cold butter into cubes and rub it into the dry ingredients until the mixture resembles coarse crumbs.
4. Pour in the cold heavy cream and quickly bring the dough together. Stir in the cranberries and chocolate chips just until combined.
5. Preheat the oven to 375°F. Shape the dough into a round disc about 1 1/2 inches (4 cm) thick and cut it into 6–8 wedges.
6. Place the scones on a parchment-lined baking sheet, spacing them apart. Bake for 20–25 minutes, until golden brown.
7. Optionally, dust with powdered sugar or drizzle with glaze.

Enjoy!

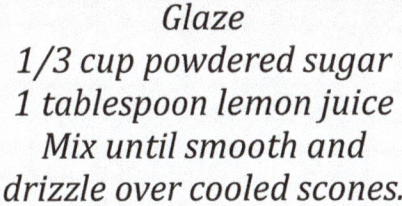

Glaze
1/3 cup powdered sugar
1 tablespoon lemon juice
Mix until smooth and drizzle over cooled scones.

Which fruit is bright orange on the outside and full of sweet, golden juice inside?

ORANGE (upside down)

Which fruit is yellow and sour, grows on a tree, and is used to make water, tea, or desserts taste extra zesty?

LEMON (upside down)

Sweet or sour words?

Oranges give sweet juice, lemons give sour juice.

People are like that too — our words are our «juice».

What kind of words do you want to share today — sweet or sour?

Let's help Toby with these puzzles!

Lemon Poppy Seed Cake

Ingredients:

- 2 cups all-purpose flour
- 4 teaspoons poppy seeds
- 1 teaspoon baking soda
- 1/2 teaspoon baking powder
- 1/4 teaspoon salt
- 1 egg
- 3/4 cup sugar
- 1/3 cup vegetable oil
- 1/3 cup sour cream or Greek yogurt
- 2/3 cup milk
- 3 tablespoons lemon juice
- 1 tablespoon lemon zest

Creative Process

1. In a large bowl, sift together the flour, poppy seeds, baking soda, baking powder, and salt.
2. In another bowl, crack the egg, add the sugar, and beat with a mixer until light and frothy.
3. Pour in the vegetable oil, sour cream (or Greek yogurt), milk, lemon juice, and lemon zest; gently mix.

4. Combine the wet ingredients with the dry ingredients and stir until just combined.
5. Preheat the oven to 350°F.
6. Grease a baking pan with oil and pour in the batter.
7. Bake for 45–50 minutes, checking doneness with a toothpick.
8. Remove the cake from the oven and let it cool completely.
9. If desired, drizzle with glaze.

Enjoy!

Glaze
1/3 cup powdered sugar
1 tablespoon lemon juice
Mix until smooth and drizzle over the cooled cake.

Let's look at this winter day.

If you could jump into this picture, where would you go first, and why?

How do you think Lily feels while she is skating — brave, a little scared, happy, or something else?

Where do you think the fox is going with the sled and presents? Who might be waiting for these gifts?

Who or what do you think Daddy Bear is taking a picture of right now?

Why do you think we like taking photos?

What do you think is in Mama Bear's basket? Who is it for?

How can you tell the grown-ups here care about the children?

If Toby and Lily told us about their favorite moment from this winter day, what do you think they would choose?

Baking with Mom Bear

What do you think Mom Bear and Toby are making with this dough?

What will happen next when the dough is ready? Tell your own ending to this story.

Look at Toby. How do you think he feels as he helps — excited, curious, proud, or something else? Why?

What is your favorite baked treat? If you were in this kitchen with Toby, what would you ask Mom Bear to bake with you?

Let's use our imagination. Look closely at the picture and see which animals you can find.
If you were a little bear, which of these forest friends would you invite over for pie?

Take a close look at the two pictures. Can you find 10 differences?

Gingerbread Christmas Tree

Ingredients:

- 3 cups all-purpose flour
- 1 teaspoon ground cinnamon
- 1 teaspoon ground ginger
- 1 1/2 teaspoons baking powder
- 9 tablespoons (127 g) butter
- 1/2 cup honey
- 1 egg
- white chocolate candy melts
- your favorite sprinkles or dried fruits and candied peel

Creative Process

1. Line a baking sheet with parchment paper.
2. In a large bowl, sift together the flour, cinnamon, ginger, and baking powder. Mix well.
3. Cut the cold butter into cubes and rub it into the dry ingredients until they resemble coarse crumbs.

4. In a small bowl, whisk the egg with the honey.
5. Pour the egg-honey mixture into the flour mixture and knead into a dough. If it's too sticky, add a little more flour.
6. Preheat the oven to 350°F.
7. On parchment paper, roll the dough 4–5 mm thick and cut out two stars of each size, leaving a small space between them. Remove any excess dough.
8. Bake for 7–9 minutes. As soon as you smell that lovely aroma, remove the cookies so they don't dry out.
9. Let the cookies cool completely.
10. Melt the white chocolate candy melts, following the package instructions.
11. Assemble a «tree pyramid»: start with the largest star at the bottom and stack the smaller ones on top, gluing them together in the center with the glaze. Decorate with sprinkles or candied fruits — press them gently into the glaze so they stay in place.

You can use this recipe to make cookies in any shape you like.

The little bears are making gingerbread cookies. Let's help them decorate! Match each silhouette to the decorated cookie.

Let's explore this picture together and find the matching pairs.
A little hint for you: 5 items are missing their pairs. Can you find them all?

Quiet time helps our thoughts settle. Everyone needs pauses. When we rest, it's like we grow a little inside and notice what truly matters.

Toby and Lily are sharing their cookies with friends.
Did everyone get the same number of treats?

Let's look at this winter night together.

What do you think the little birds are whispering to each other on the snowy branch?

How do you think Papa Bear feels while pulling the tree — proud, excited, or a little tired?

If you were here, where would you sit — on the sled, on the branch, or in the soft snow? Why?

What feelings do you think the little bears have while Papa Bear pulls the sled?

If you could ask Papa Bear one big or small question, what would it be?

What do you imagine the bears will do as soon as they reach their cozy home?

What holiday tradition do you notice in this picture?

What traditions does your family enjoy during this season?

What do you imagine is inside these presents, and who might they be for?

And if one gift were for you, what would you wish to find inside?

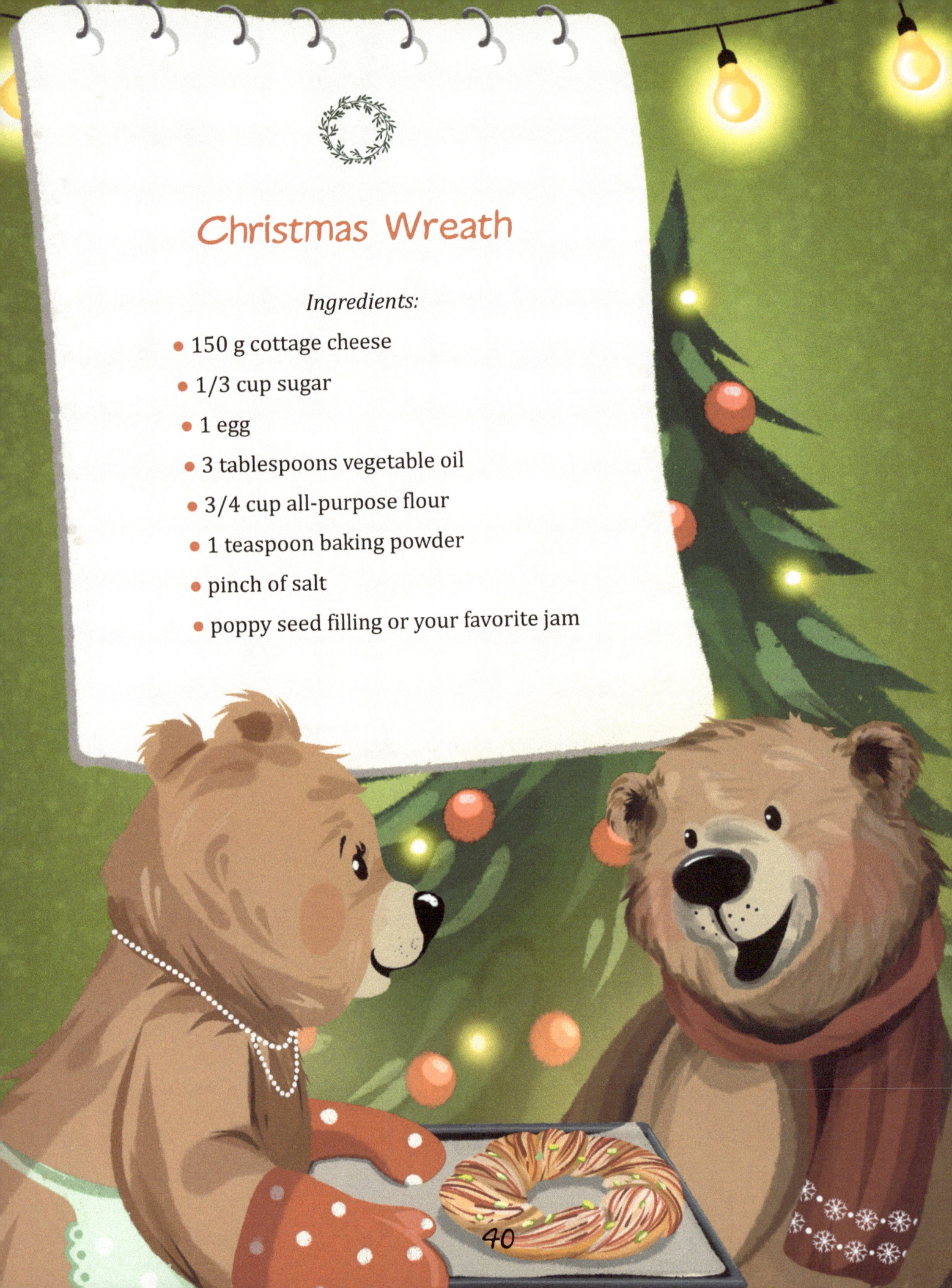

Christmas Wreath

Ingredients:

- 150 g cottage cheese
- 1/3 cup sugar
- 1 egg
- 3 tablespoons vegetable oil
- 3/4 cup all-purpose flour
- 1 teaspoon baking powder
- pinch of salt
- poppy seed filling or your favorite jam

Creative Process

1. In a large bowl, combine the cottage cheese, sugar, egg, oil, and salt.
2. Sift in the flour and baking powder, then knead into a soft dough. Add a little extra flour if the dough feels too sticky.
3. Preheat your oven to 355°F.
4. Roll the dough into a rectangle, spread the filling evenly, and roll it up into a log.

5. Slice the log lengthwise, then gently twist the two halves together to form a wreath. Sprinkle with chopped nuts if you like.
6. Place the wreath on a baking sheet and bake for about 40 minutes. Remove from the oven, let it cool slightly, and slice.

You can substitute avocado with ripe bananas (1 cup), but you'll need to add 2–3 tablespoons of vegetable oil and reduce the sugar to 1/2 cup.

Festive Brownies

Ingredients:
- 2 medium ripe avocados (≈1 cup mashed)
- 1 cup coconut or light brown sugar
- 1/2 cup unsweetened cocoa powder
- 3 large eggs
- 1/2 cup brown rice flour
- 1/2 teaspoon baking soda
- pinch of salt
- 1 teaspoon vanilla extract
- 1/2 cup chocolate chips

For decorating:
- chocolate candy melts
- candy cane or short pretzel stick
- sprinkles

Creative Process

1. Preheat the oven to 350°F.
2. Halve, pit, and peel the avocados. Mash to a smooth purée, then beat in the sugar.
3. While beating, add the eggs one at a time, then the vanilla extract.
4. In a separate bowl, whisk together the cocoa powder, rice flour, baking soda, and salt.
5. Fold the dry ingredients into the avocado mixture until just combined.
6. Gently stir in the chocolate chips.

7. Line an 8 × 8 inch baking pan with parchment paper; pour in the batter.
8. Bake for 25–30 minutes, until a skewer comes out with just a few moist crumbs (no raw batter).
9. Let the brownies cool in the pan for at least 30 minutes, then transfer to a board and cut into triangles.

10. Melt the chocolate glaze, fill a piping bag, snip off the tip, and pipe the green glaze onto each brownie triangle (see illustration). Top with sprinkles and insert a little «trunk».

Enjoy your festive treat!

Chocolate Christmas Trees

Ingredients:

- 15 savory or sweet stick cookies (twists)
- 1 cup green chocolate candy melts
- sprinkles

Feel free to use candy melts in any color, and replace the cookie stick with a plastic or wooden stick if needed.

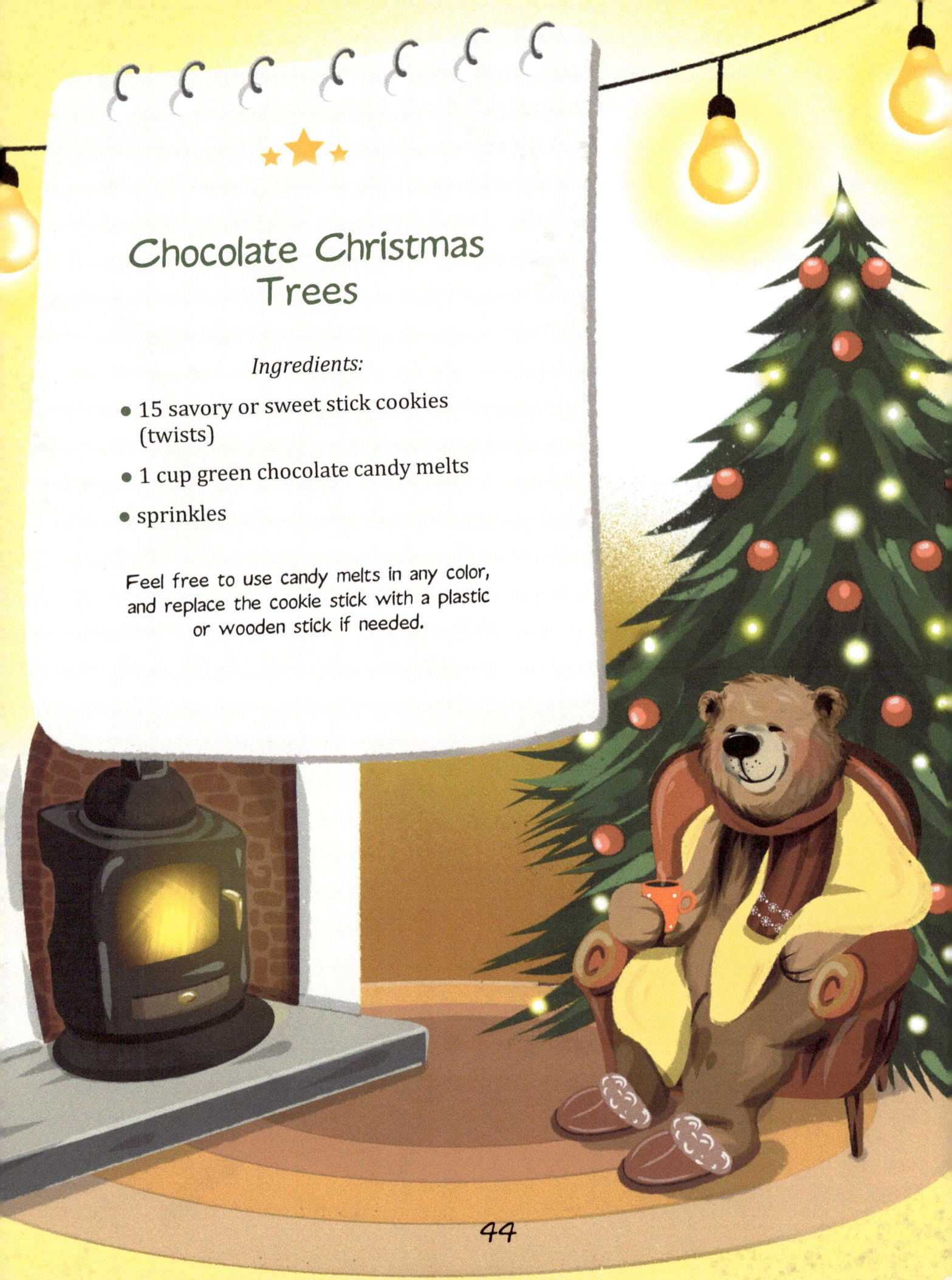

Creative Process

1. Line a board with plastic wrap or parchment paper and place the sticks, spacing them 2–3 inches apart.
2. Melt the chocolate candy melts according to the package instructions.
3. Fill a pastry bag with the melted coating and snip off the tip.
4. Pipe small tree shapes onto each stick.
5. Immediately decorate with sprinkles and let fully set.

These chocolate trees make a wonderful decoration for a holiday cake or cupcakes.

Christmas wreath shortbread cookies

Ingredients:

- 1/3 cup sugar + 1 tablespoon
- pinch of salt
- 11 teaspoons (~150 g) softened butter
- 1 egg
- 2 cups all-purpose flour
- 1 teaspoon baking powder
- 1 egg white for brushing
- about 150 g pistachios and dried fruits, roughly chopped

In the original version, the cookies are garnished with finely chopped peanuts.

Creative Process

1. In a large bowl, cream the sugar, salt, and softened butter with a mixer for 3 minutes, until light and fluffy.
2. Add the egg and beat for another minute to fully incorporate.
3. Sift in the flour and baking powder, then mix until a soft dough forms. If the dough feels too loose, add a bit more flour.
4. Wrap the dough in plastic wrap and chill in the refrigerator for 30 minutes.

5. Preheat the oven to 350°F.
6. Using a knife, finely chop the pistachios and dried fruits; set aside.
7. Separate the egg white from the yolk, and lightly beat the white in a small bowl with a fork.
8. Lightly dust a baking sheet with flour. Roll out the dough, cut out circles with a cookie cutter, then use a smaller cutter to remove the center of each circle and form rings.

9. Brush each ring with the beaten egg white, then evenly sprinkle with the chopped pistachios and dried fruits.
10. Bake for 15 minutes, or until the cookies turn a light golden brown. Remove from the oven and allow them to cool completely.

Enjoy!

Take a close look at the two pictures.
Can you find 10 differences?

Look up at the sky, my sweethearts.
See that star — the very first one tonight.
They say that if you whisper a wish when it appears,
a quiet little wonder drifts into your heart —
as if the sky whispered back.

A long time ago,
a very special star lit up the night —
the one that showed the way to baby Jesus.
It was a gift of hope for the whole world.

And every star that shines after that
is like a gentle reminder:
«Love is near. God is near».

Sometimes, a feeling lives in your heart —
something quiet… not easy to explain, but very real.
Maybe a wish. Or a thought. Or a little dream.
You can tell it to God — He always listens.
And everything that matters to you…
matters to Him too.
We're never alone.
I love thinking about that.

And now, my dear ones, it's time to sleep…
May your dreams be soft,
your blanket warm,
and your heart full of light.

God bless this night and all of us…
Sweet dreams!

Star light, star bright,
First star I see tonight,
I wish I may,
I wish I might,
Have the wish I wish tonight.

Chocolate Crinkle Cookies

Ingredients:

- 1 + 1/4 cups all-purpose flour
- 1/3 + 1/3 cup cocoa powder
- 1 teaspoon baking powder
- pinch of salt
- 2 cups powdered sugar
- 1/4 cup (60 g) unsalted butter
- 2 eggs
- 1 cup powdered sugar for rolling

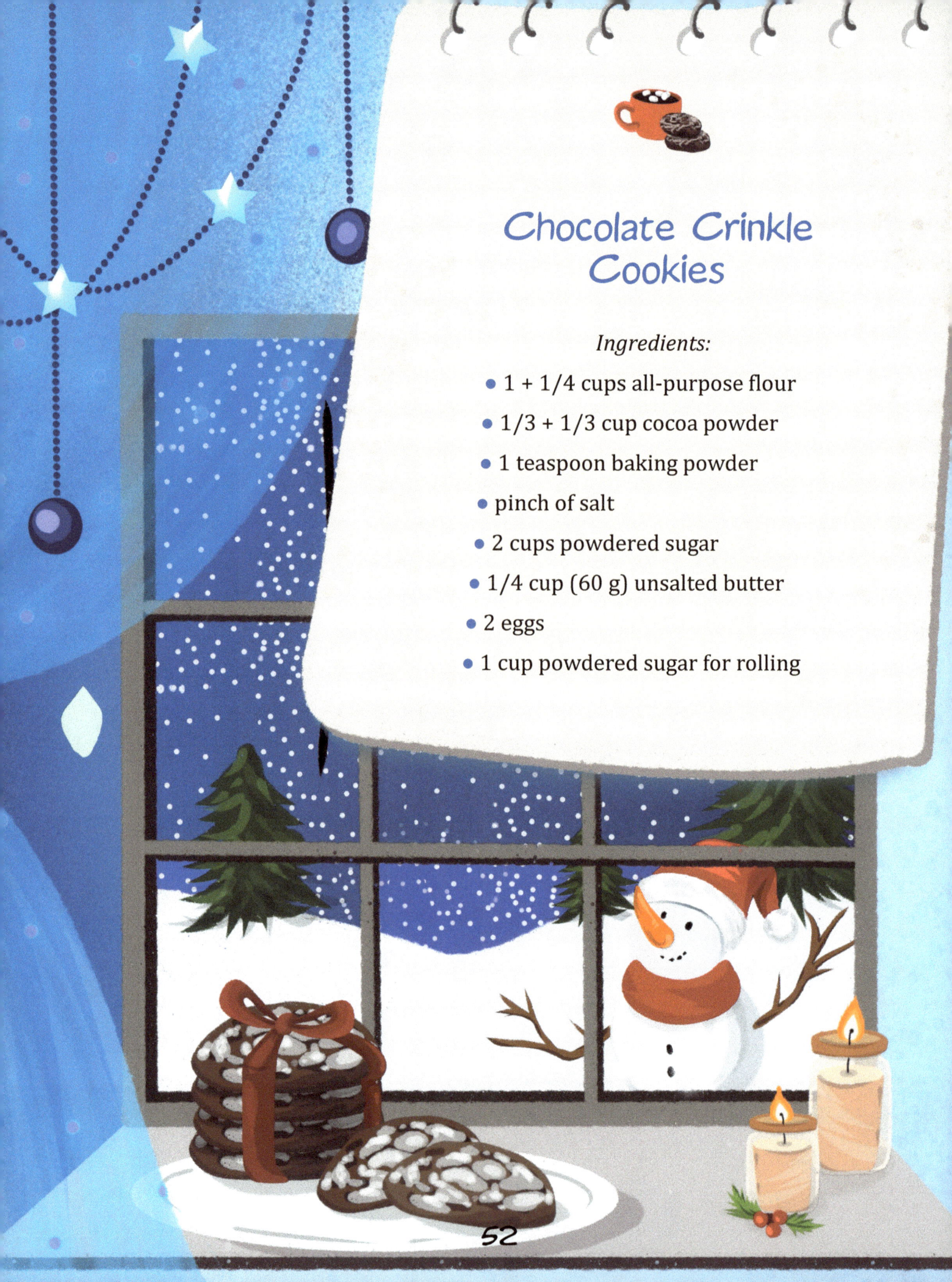

Creative Process

1. In a large bowl, sift together the flour, cocoa powder, baking powder, salt, and 2 cups of powdered sugar.

2. Cut the cold butter into small pieces, add it to the dry ingredients, and rub it in with your fingers until the mixture looks like fine crumbs.

3. In a separate bowl, lightly beat the eggs, then add them to the dough and mix until fully combined.

4. Cover the bowl with plastic wrap and chill the dough in the refrigerator for 30 minutes.

5. Place the remaining 1 cup of powdered sugar into a small bowl for rolling.

6. Preheat the oven to 350°F (175°C).

7. Remove the dough from the refrigerator. Pinch off small walnut-sized portions, roll them into balls, and coat each one generously in the powdered sugar.

8. Place the balls on a parchment-lined baking sheet, spacing them about 2 inches apart. Bake for 10–12 minutes.

9. Remove the cookies from the oven and let them cool on the baking sheet, then transfer them to a plate. Serve and enjoy!

Enjoy your tea time!

I get hot, but I don't burn myself.
You open my door to check on cookies.
I bake and roast — what am I?

OVEN

I cook food very fast, using steam and pressure.
You have to be careful when opening me.
I hiss and make noise — what am I?

PRESSURE COOKER

I wear pots and pans like hats.
I make water boil and soup bubble.
I have burners but no flames in my heart — what am I?

STOVE

I sing when I'm ready.
You fill me with water, and I make it hot.
People use me for tea — what am I?

KETTLE

I make bread jump when it's ready.
I like things golden and crispy.
Put slices in, and I'll pop them out — what am I?

TOASTER

I spin and chop and slice in seconds.
You feed me veggies, and I turn them into pieces.
I can mix, but I'm not a blender — what am I?

FOOD PROCESSOR

I don't like warmth.
I keep food cold and safe.
I have a light inside, and I hum softly — what am I?

REFRIGERATOR

Let's imagine!
What do you think the bear cubs could eat for breakfast today?
Or for lunch? Maybe even for a snack or dinner?

Cranberry Chocolate Chip Cookies

Ingredients:

- 1/2 cup (113 g) soft unsalted butter
- 1/2 cup sugar
- 1 egg
- 1 teaspoon vanilla
- 1 1/2 cups all-purpose flour
- 1/2 teaspoon baking soda
- 1 teaspoon lemon juice or vinegar
- 1/2 cup chocolate chips
- 1 cup dried cranberries

Creative Process

1. In a large bowl, cream together the softened butter and sugar. Add the egg and vanilla extract, and mix until smooth.
2. Add the flour and baking soda (pre-activated with lemon juice or vinegar), stirring until a soft dough forms.
3. Gently fold in the chocolate chips and dried cranberries.
4. Portion the dough into walnut-sized balls, shape into rounds, and lightly flatten them.
5. Preheat the oven to 375°F. Arrange the cookies on a parchment-lined baking sheet, spacing them 2–3 cm apart.
6. Bake for about 15 minutes, until the edges are lightly golden. Remove from the oven and let the cookies cool completely.

Enjoy!

Try your own mix-ins — chocolate, raisins, or cranberries!

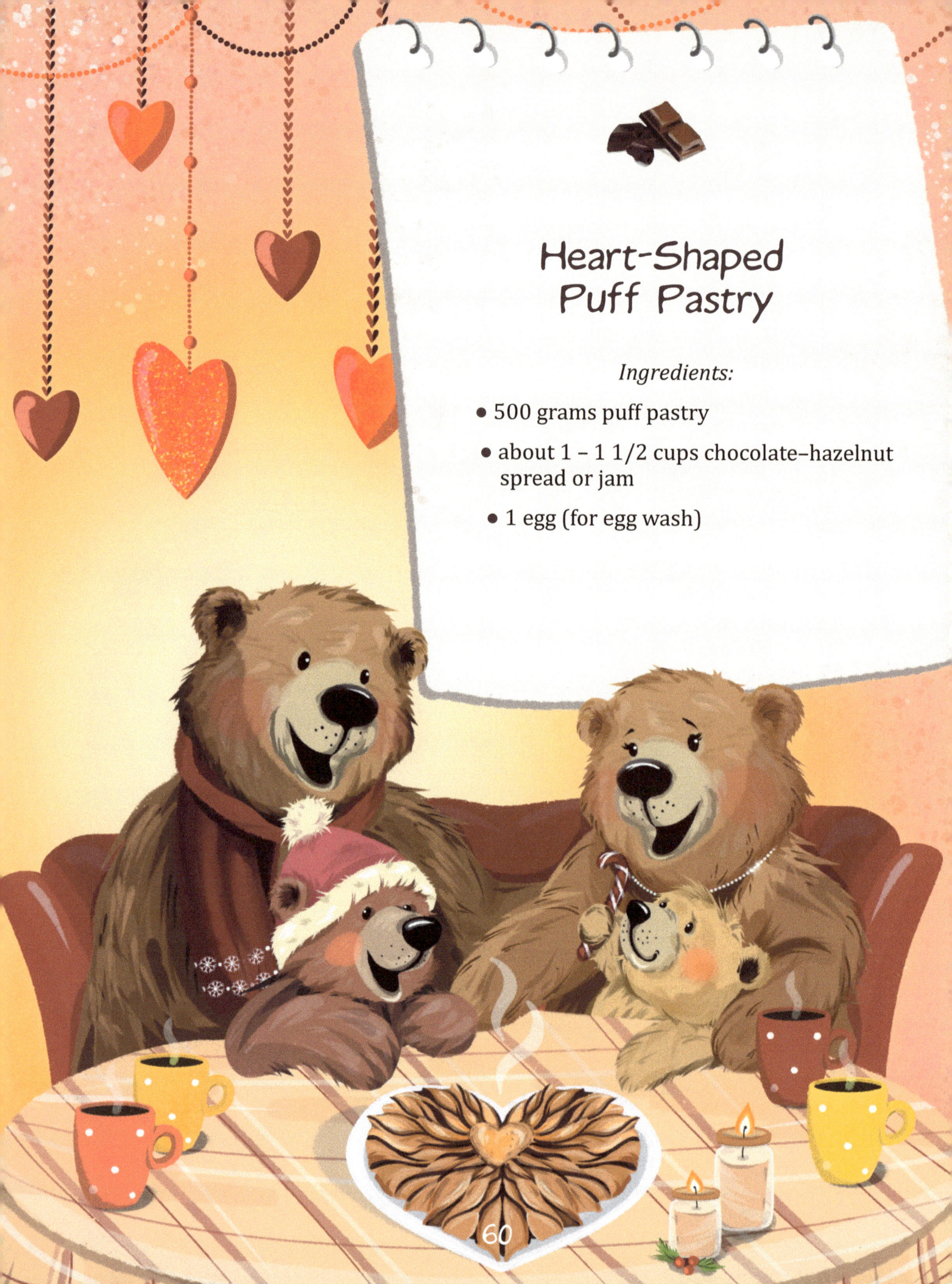

Heart-Shaped Puff Pastry

Ingredients:

- 500 grams puff pastry
- about 1 – 1 1/2 cups chocolate-hazelnut spread or jam
- 1 egg (for egg wash)

Creative Process

1. Thaw the puff pastry according to the package instructions.
2. Lightly dust your work surface with flour and roll the dough out slightly.
3. Cut out two large heart shapes using a cookie cutter or a knife. Spread the filling over one heart, then place the second heart on top.

4. Press a small cookie cutter or the rim of a glass into the center (without cutting all the way through) to mark a heart or circle. From this outline, slice the outer dough into «rays», then twist each strip into a spiral.
5. In a small bowl, beat the egg with a fork and brush it over the top of the pastry hearts.

6. Preheat the oven to 390°F. Bake on a parchment-lined sheet for 20–25 minutes, until golden brown.

Enjoy!

There is love in every heart. But everyone feels and shows love in their own special way. These ways are called «love languages».
There are five of them: hugs, kind words, gifts, helping, and spending time together.
Let's discover which love languages the bear family speaks!

Toby loves hugs the most.
That's how he feels best and how he says «I love you» without words.

Which path will Toby take to go give Mama a hug?

Lily feels love through words.
She loves hearing kind phrases — thank-yous, compliments,
and little encouragements.
And it's easy for her to share love the same way —
with sweet words from her heart.

Let's read these kind phrases — and maybe come up with a few new ones together!

Helping and caring — that's Mama Bear's love language.
Lily and Toby want to say «I love you» in her language.
While Mama is having her tea, Toby dusts the shelves,
and Lily is tidying up the kitchen cupboard.

What's out of place on the shelves? Let's help put everything where it belongs!

For Daddy Bear, love means spending time together —
just the two of them, the three of them, or the whole family.
When everyone cooks something tasty together, it feels extra special.
Let's look at the pictures and find five differences!

What are some other ways to spend time as a family?

Grandma Bear speaks the language of gifts.
Toby and Lily have prepared something special just for her.
Let's help them deliver their gift with love:
follow the colored path 💚💛❤️ to find out which house she lives in.

If we want someone to truly hear our «I love you»,
it helps to say it in their own love language.

Let's learn how to fold a napkin into a heart. and decorate the festive table with it.

Let all that you do be done in love.

Using short pieces of string, pencils, or toothpicks, let's connect the matching pairs of gingerbread cookies!

Berry & Almond Loaf Cake

Ingredients:

- zest of 1 orange
- 5 eggs
- 1 teaspoon vanilla extract
- 1/2 cup sugar or sugar substitute
- 3 tablespoons cream
- 3 tablespoons butter or coconut oil
- 2 cups almond flour
- 2 tablespoons coconut flour
- 1 1/2 teaspoons baking powder
- 1/2 cup fresh or frozen cranberries

You can also make this cake with blueberries for a delicious variation.

Creative Process

1. Grease a loaf pan with oil.
2. Wash the orange and finely grate its zest.
3. Preheat the oven to 350°F.
4. In a large bowl, beat the eggs, vanilla extract, and sugar (or substitute) with a mixer for 2–3 minutes.
5. Add the cream and softened butter, then beat for another minute.
6. In a separate bowl, whisk together the almond flour, coconut flour, and baking powder. Gently fold this mixture into the egg mixture until just combined.
7. Stir in the cranberries and orange zest. Pour the batter into the prepared pan.
8. Bake for 45–50 minutes, or until a skewer inserted into the center comes out clean. Remove from the oven and let the cake cool in the pan for 10–15 minutes.
9. Optionally, drizzle with white icing or dust with icing sugar.

Enjoy!

Don't have a Bundt pan? A regular loaf pan works just fine.

When we finish an activity, we clean up. It's a gentle way of caring for our home and each other. It also makes our space ready for the next little adventure.

Let's look at the pictures together! What did she do first? What happened second? What did she do after that?

Dinner is a special time in the bear family. It's not only about tasty food — it's also about warm conversations, when everyone can gently share how their day went and truly listen to one another.

It feels so good to tell your family what matters to you — what you saw, heard, felt, learned, or did today;
what made you happy or a little sad;
what surprised you, what you handled well, and what didn't go quite as planned...

It's wonderful when family is a place where you feel understood and accepted — where you can be yourself, feel loved, and give love in return.

When do you feel most loved?

What does love mean to you?

What does it feel like?

Let's read the happiness recipe shared by the bear family — and then try to make our own!

Recipe for Happiness

Ingredients:

- 2 cups of kind words
- 3 tablespoons of warm hugs
- 1 cup of time together
- 5 teaspoons of help and care
- 2 small gifts from the heart

Creative Process

1. Gently pour in the kind words — they make everything feel cozy. Sift them through honesty and kindness.
2. Mix in hugs and smiles, slowly and warmly, until the mixture feels soft and comforting.
3. Add time spent together — it helps the happiness grow!
4. Sprinkle in help and care — they bring a special flavor.
5. Decorate with tiny gifts — even a small drawing or note can make happiness shine.
6. Bake it all with love and thankfulness. Check with your heart: if it feels joyful and calm — it's ready!

Enjoy your beautiful life!

Tropical Winter Loaf Cake

Ingredients:
- 3 cups all-purpose flour
- 1/2 teaspoon salt
- 1 teaspoon baking soda
- 2 cups sugar
- 1/2 teaspoon ground cinnamon
- 1/2 teaspoon ground ginger
- 1/2 teaspoon ground nutmeg
- 1 cup chopped walnuts
- 3 eggs, lightly beaten
- 1 cup vegetable oil
- 2 cups ripe banana purée (mashed bananas)
- 1 can (230 g) pineapple chunks
- 2 teaspoons vanilla extract
- 1 cup shredded coconut
- 1 cup total of dried cherries, cranberries, and candied fruit

Creative Process

1. Grease two 9 × 5 inch loaf pans with butter or oil.
2. Preheat the oven to 350°F.
3. In a large bowl, sift together the flour, salt, baking soda, sugar, and spices (cinnamon, ginger, nutmeg). Mix well.
4. Add the remaining ingredients and stir until just combined — try not to overmix.
5. Divide the batter between the pans and bake for 45–50 minutes. Check for doneness with a toothpick: it should come out clean from the center.
6. Remove from the oven and let the loaves cool in the pans for 10–15 minutes. Then transfer to a wire rack and slice once fully cooled.

Enjoy your treat!

Optional: Dust with powdered sugar or drizzle with glaze. You can also garnish with fresh fruit pieces.

Pat-a-cake, pat-a-cake, baker's man,
bake me a cake as fast as you can;
pat it and prick it, and mark it with t,
put it in the oven for Toby and me.

Did you know, little one?

A long time ago, families used big ovens to bake their pies together.

So they marked each one with a letter — just like we did today — to tell whose was whose!

And back then, the word cake meant all kinds of baked goodies — even cookies like ours!

Let's find the first letter of your name!
(And mommy's letter... And daddy's...)

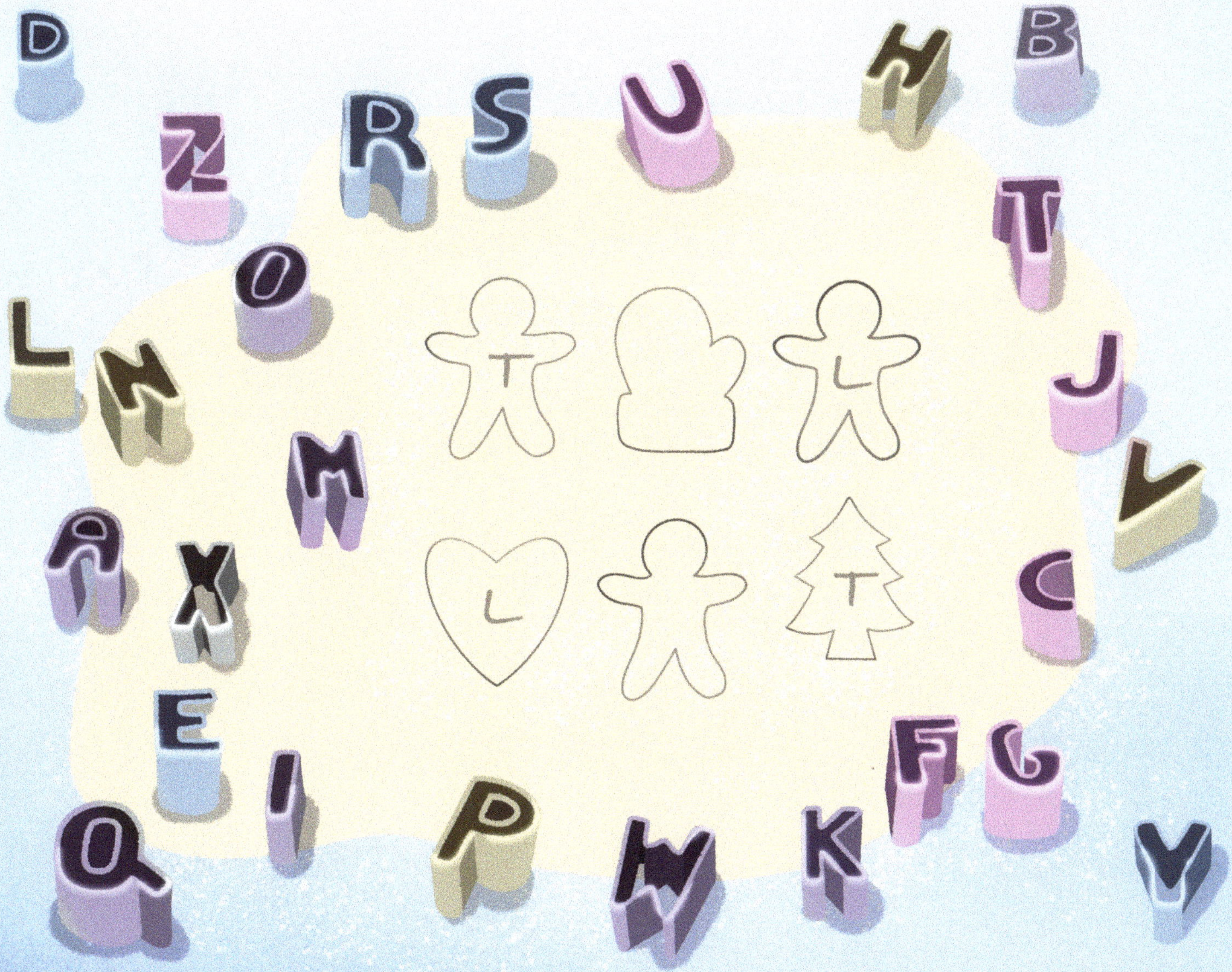

Sometimes we're in such a hurry that we forget
to see all the good things around us.
But little wonders happen every day —
we just need to stop and notice them.

True happiness is learning to notice
blessings every day.

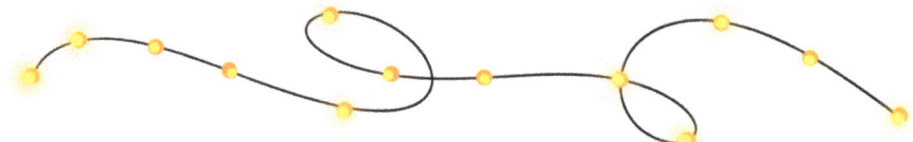

PARENTS' PAGES

Dear Parents, I'm so happy we've met 🙂

And even happier that this book is already in your hands.

I truly believe that the ideas on these pages will inspire you to create together — and that the result will be not only delicious pastries, but also a deep emotional connection: a feeling of closeness with yourself and with your child.

Let these 13 recipes — along with illustrations, poems, riddles, mazes, and other activities — be a gentle bridge toward that closeness.

May they support heart-to-heart conversations and bring harmony into your home, so that both parenting and childhood can feel like joy. 🙏

This winter book is the first in a series covering all four seasons.

Its central theme is family and shared time as a precious value.

The heartfelt illustrations of a bear family gently remind us of what truly matters.

Within its pages, you'll also find a whole section dedicated to love.

Inspired by Gary Chapman's The 5 Love Languages, I wanted to highlight the many ways this great feeling can be expressed.

Understanding those differences helps us listen — to ourselves and to one another — and grow closer.

This book is a gentle reminder to slow down, to pause, and to listen to the quiet within — a place from which joy and clarity can emerge... and life begins to feel more in order, more peaceful.

You'll also find many cozy winter and Christmas-themed pages filled with light and warmth — much like the art of my favorite painter, Thomas Kinkade.

May the warmth and harmony of this book fill your home and remind you of your own inner glow — and the Source of all true light. 🙏

On these pages, you'll find a small exercise that engages both hemispheres of the brain at once.

It may look simple, but it helps children develop coordination and focus in a playful way.

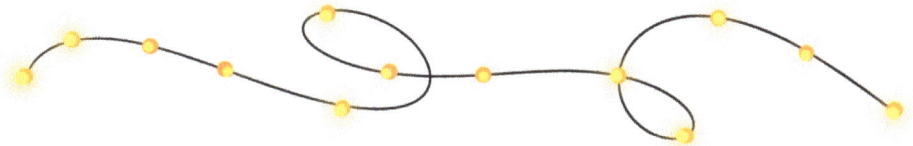

You can even try a similar trick in the kitchen — let your child stir in two bowls at the same time using both hands.

Little moments like these gently support balanced brain development.

Now I'd love to share — gently — what helps me cook joyfully with children:

1. Create a sense of intention.

In any activity — especially in parenting — intention matters. Ask yourself: Why am I doing this? What do I want my child to feel or learn? What is my long-term goal?

When I return to these core questions — connection, presence, love — the stress melts away, and everything becomes more meaningful.

Emotional connection works better than any reward or punishment.

When both of you value that connection, it becomes much easier to choose actions that lead to true cooperation.

2. Choose the right moment.

It's not only about having all the ingredients — it's also about checking in with yourself and your child. Hunger, tiredness, or overstimulation can easily spoil even the coziest recipe.

Choosing a day ahead of time, finding one quiet hour — without rush — helps everyone truly enjoy the process. That creates rhythm, and rhythm gives us inner stability.

3. Gently tune in to your child.

Washing hands, putting on an apron — these simple steps already create togetherness.

Soft xylophone sounds, a finger play, a short melody or prayer — these tiny rituals gently whisper: «We're here together. I see you. I'm with you».

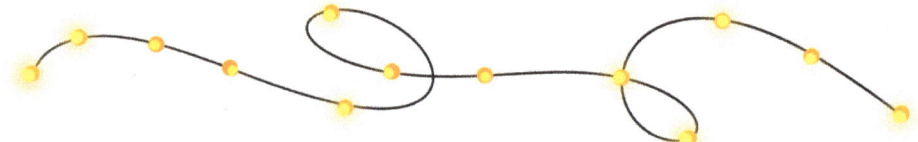

4. Cook not for your child, but with them.

Cooking with a child keeps me connected to myself. Children sense our authenticity — if I enjoy the moment, they are naturally drawn in. If I don't, they drift away. (Just like in Tom Sawyer painting the fence — remember?)

This book was created in the spirit of collaboration — even the recipes gently remind the adult: «We are building connection».

5. The 3s rule: slowly, step-by-step, steadily.

This is a gentle reminder — for myself and the child — to be kind, not to expect too much too soon, and to start with simple steps and simple recipes...

6. Create a cozy kind of silence.

Try not to become an endless stream of instructions.

Children need pauses — to process, to absorb, to wonder.

Those quiet moments, when they fall into the rhythm of the task, are truly precious.

7. Gentle guidance instead of control.

The more wisely we organize the space and tasks, the freer the child feels.

When we offer them «just right» responsibilities, they grow in confidence: «I can do it. I'm learning. I'm capable».

Look for what's going well. Point out their strengths, their ideas, their effort — with words like: «Your fingers seem to love kneading this dough».

That builds inner awareness — and feels much better than correction. 🙂

8. Use songs, rhymes, riddles and poems.

These are powerful tools in kitchen rituals: a song makes cleanup more fun, a rhyme can assign roles or colors, a poem or riddle can introduce the dish you're about to make.

And it's not just fun — it supports language, rhythm, and memory. It brings soul to the routine.

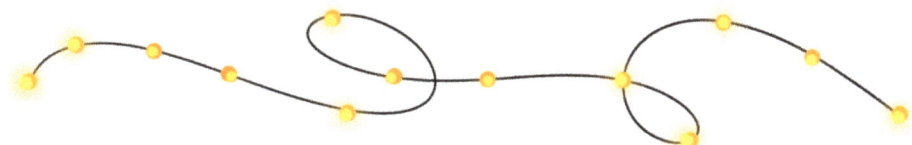

9. Leaving room for imagination and creativity.

Following a recipe is an important life skill. At the same time, cooking offers space for creativity.

We don't let children mix ingredients randomly, because we teach care, respect for food, and mindful use of ingredients.

But creativity comes through other parts of cooking — choosing shapes, trying different fillings or spices, and decorating cookies or cupcakes. Children can start by copying your example and then add their own ideas.

We can also nurture imagination through beautiful presentation: setting the table, folding napkins, or adding simple decorations.

10. Let go of rushing. Value the child's pace and initiative.

Children aged 3 to 7 often want to do everything — but they do it more slowly... Let's give them time to grow in their own rhythm — without hurrying, without correcting every little thing. And may their initiative never be punished.

11. Anchor the positive emotion.

When everything flows well — a child will naturally want to return: «Let's do this again!» One helpful tip: divide complex recipes into steps. Knead the dough in the morning — decorate cookies later. The younger the child, the more we break the process down into joyful «tastes». In the beginning, they might just want to be nearby. Let them. That time will naturally grow as they do.

And yes — the recipes are designed to help. All the recipes in this book have been tested — by me, and by many little chefs in both home and preschool kitchens. So I warmly invite you into this world of culinary creativity!

May this book be not just a collection of recipes — but a meeting place for you and your child... 🙏

With love,
Nataliia Prokopchik

Acknowledgments

My deepest gratitude goes to my beloved husband, Yuri Prokopchik, for supporting my ideas on every level and creating the conditions that made this project possible.

My heartfelt thanks to the talented illustrator, Anastasiia Zhelik, for bringing to life the warm and cozy images that so precisely reflect everything I had envisioned and dreamed of.

Warm thanks to our book designer, Oleksandr Dubasov, for his professional work and harmonious page layouts.

My sincere gratitude goes to my wonderful community — my family and children. It is they who inspired me to create this project.

A big thank-you to the parents of my young chefs for their trust and for recognizing the value of our culinary sessions.

I am grateful to my teachers, mentors, and guides whose personal example, encouragement, and support shaped my professional growth — especially Iryna Stetsenko, Olga Melnyk and Olena Polovina.

My special thanks to Shalva Amonashvili for the pedagogical wisdom I had the privilege to encounter through his lectures, and for the many books that became a source of inspiration, strength, and guidance in my work.

I am deeply thankful to my wonderful parents, Vasyl and Tetiana Korba, for the gift of life and for their heartfelt prayers.

I am grateful to the Creator for creativity itself, for all talents and possibilities, and for the great gift of loving people.

And finally — thank you, my dear readers! I wish you a joyful childhood, joyful parenthood, and countless heart-warming moments with your little ones. May you «cook» happiness together and savor every bit of it.

With love and gratitude,
Nataliia

ABOUT THE AUTHOR

Nataliia Prokopchik comes from Kamianets-Podilskyi — one of Ukraine's most picturesque cities, known for its medieval fortress and rich cultural heritage.

She is an early childhood educator and a graduate of the National Pedagogical Dragomanov University (Kyiv, Ukraine).

Nataliia is the author of the book «Cooking with Children, or Something More», as well as articles published in professional journals.

She has over ten years of experience leading culinary activities for children — first in Ukraine, at an early-development center and at a private school and later in Sacramento, California, where she moved in 2016.

Now living in Las Vegas, Nevada, she continues to promote cooking as a powerful educational tool that nurtures inner harmony and supports a child's growth.

Nataliia calls herself a gourmet of the moment. She sees life as a spiritual kitchen where, together with the Head Chef, we «cook» our everyday stories. We have been gifted the freedom to choose our own «ingredients» — and all the tools we need to savor life's many «flavors».

To be a gourmet of life means to live with deep attentiveness, to pause, to feel grateful, and to delight in His grace.

To learn more about her books, classes, and projects, please visit

www.natawithkids.com

Cook every day of your life with love

www.ingramcontent.com/pod-product-compliance
Lightning Source LLC
Chambersburg PA
CBHW051325110526
44582CB00004B/104